THE HEART OF DIGNITY

ELLA JEAN JACKSON

Author's Tranquility Press
MARRIETTA, GEORGIA

Copyright © 2022 by Ella Jean Jackson.

All rights reserved. No part of this publication may be reproduced, distributed or transmitted in any form or by any means, including photocopying, recording, or other electronic or mechanical methods, without the prior written permission of the publisher, except in the case of brief quotations embodied in critical reviews and certain other noncommercial uses permitted by copyright law. For permission requests, write to the publisher, addressed "Attention: Permissions Coordinator," at the address below.

Ella Jean Jackson/Author's Tranquility Press
2706 Station Club Drive SW
Marietta, GA 30060
www.authorstranquilitypress.com

Publisher's Note: This is a work of fiction. Names, characters, places, and incidents are a product of the author's imagination. Locales and public names are sometimes used for atmospheric purposes. Any resemblance to actual people, living or dead, or to businesses, companies, events, institutions, or locales is completely coincidental.

Ordering Information:
Quantity sales. Special discounts are available on quantity purchases by corporations, associations, and others. For details, contact the "Special Sales Department" at the address above.

The Heart of Dignity/Ella Jean Jackson
Paperback: 978-1-957208-37-4
eBook: 978-1-957208-43-5

Peace, Joy, and Happiness with blessing all around

DEDICATION

To All the folks who believed in me with motivation. He is a very kind man who I admire. He has given me the name Cristina. God is in control of all things. God has eternal love for me and my family. I am proud of my Mom who had raised a grateful young lady. I also have two sisters and three brothers. The best is yet to come. You are the best and the world has yet to see you. To my two handsome sons, four grand Kids whose expectation of me causes me to continuously look to God for more strength when I feel like I can't go on. Because you are, I must be, I must do, and I must achieve so I will always know that through Christ, all things are possible and in him I also will be, will do, and will achieve. A mother and a lady who is a warrior.

Thank You

To God who in not only the author and finisher of my faith, strength, and knowledge but is truly the author of this book. Nothing too big, impossible and impossible for God. To the ones who stood by me through thick and thin when my back was against the wall. And who have consistently spoken life into my life.

The Surviving Heart

In many days I have learned the true meaning of the verse of scripture that says" In everything give thanks to the lord for this is the will of God in Christ Jesus concerning you" (I THESSALONIANS 5:18). As I am writing, I am in the process of receiving a spiritual promotion, just as many of you who sit and read these words right now are in the midst of moving to the next dimension in life. The words, the thoughts, and my secrets. They are externally etched there through experiences and revelation that was the experiences were good, some were not so good, and many were terrible. But they all helped to bring forth lessons and revelation that God would have me to learn for the making of me, and the edifying of you. My earnest desire is that you will receive the treasure of my heart. That you will receive in the spirit that I give it to you and that you would, without hesitation, delve into the thoughts of my heart that I will share with you and ultimately allow them to help you grasp the importance of that critical time you are in why folks must go through go what you are going through and why folks must go through it with praise in the mouth and humbleness in my heart. Learn from what folks say and you will be blessed. These are the Inscriptions of my heart and soul.

INTRODUCTION

As I sit and begin to write this book, it is not reluctantly, but it is with mixed emotions and pain. It is not with some great outline, syllabus, or plan that I begin this awesome task, but simply in obedience to the voice of my lord God that said" It is that time to get started writing. For some time now there has been a deep desire within me to write the sentiments of my heart. Furthermore, the word of God has come. Many times, in the last couple of years saying, "write your book." However, there was always something to stop it. This was the most challenging times of my life. God had wanted me to know that even in this time of great challenge and trail in my life, his hand was on me. His spirit was with me and because of my faithfulness, there was a new level of anointing that was about to overtake me. I have been seeking God for it through prayer and consecration, but this was my time and what I'd been after spiritually was due to me at this moment. So not in a church service, Community, or some other form of public organized worship or man that my new anointing was released to me. But because of a sincere heart and a kept promise, in the quiet of my living room in the middle of the day on April 26, 2016.

The life of Cristina Jesus Christ. I give all my thanks to my God. Let me please start out by giving my thanks to the good Lord and my family. If it was not for the good Lord, I would not be here today. God could have given up on me a long time ago. I thank God for being there for me. I would not have made it this far if it was not for the good Lord. If you ever feel like giving up, you just have to go to God not man. Man can't never help you. I tried man several times, but none of it worked never left my side. God had surrounded me with his angles at all times and he had protected me from my enemies from Psalm 91. I will start by saying thank you for reading and buying my book. The story needs to be told. I will tell about my life story. This is where my story begins. Me and my father was born in a small town in Mississippi. My mother is from New Orleans. My father had gotten tired of Mississippi. He had stopped his education when he was in the 8th grade. My mother had graduated from 12th grade. She did not receive a high school diploma at that present moment or year. During those times, they didn't have any upgrade stuff like today. My father was married twice. My mother was married once. My father had met my mother when she was only eighteen years old. My father was twenty-four years old at that time. My father had told me once before the he had always had taken me, my sister and brothers to Mississippi every weekend. I had stayed with my grandmother until I was ten years of age. She had died so I had to return back to New Orleans. I had cried because I did not want to go back to New Orleans. New Orleans was too fast for me. I was a country girl which I had loved to be. My father had died after Katrina December 4th, 2005. My father had died at the age of 65. My mother is 71 years of age at the moment. She will be 72 June 5th God spare life. I Cristina fifty- one years of age. My mother had six children by my dad. She had three girls and three boys. All of us are still living. My mother was still a virgin until 18 years of age. My father had a son. My mother and father had adopted my stepbrother. My brother had gotten killed at the age of 19th• My stepbrother and I was in the country by my grandmother before she had passed away. My brother, me and my sister had gone to an elementary on Colisium St. After elementary school we had went to a middle school. My stepbrother had gone to college. My stepbrother had stopped in the 11th grade. My sister Rita had stopped in the 12th grade. My sister Sonia had graduated from the 12th grade. My brothers had all had graduated from the 12th grade. I Cristina is the only one that had graduated from the 12th grade, B.S., and a Master Degree in Business Administration. I had come a long way. You all just wait until I get to the real life story. I Cristina had graduated from Senior High in 1983. I also had graduated from a university in 2005. That was the biggest class ever. I give all of my thanks to God in heaven, and also to my dad and mom. My dad and mom had always have encouraged me to keep my head up no matter what happens. I am ready to tell my story now. I had just had wanted to start my back out with my profile. I had started working when I was five years old in the fields picking cotton field peas, red beans and rice. When I had moved to New

Orleans, I had started working in a grocery store. Me and my sisters and brothers were picking up trash. We were only getting paid a dollar a piece. During those days that was a lot of money. My mother was staying in the Saint Thomas projects.

My mother had moved into the Saint Thomas Project when I, Cristina at the age of ten years old. My stepbrother was sixth teen years old. My stepbrother was selling drugs at that time. I didn't expose this information until he had gotten killed. I had to wonder why everyone was treating me like a queen in the project. My stepbrother was a kingpin. Every time I would walk the streets everyone would move on the side and let me pass by. I had felt good about being treated that way. I was just too young to understand what was going on at that time. But now I know the real reason why I was treated with respect in that way. That was not the right way to earn respect. This is where my stepbrother life had ended. Three days before Father's Day in 1979 a young man had come and had knocked on my mother's door. He had called my stepbrother by bullet proof. I had said that he was asleep. I had never seen that young man before. He had said go and wake his punk ass up. I had gone upstairs to wake up. I had tried to shake him, but nothing had worked. When I had come back downstairs the young man had disappeared. When my brother had finally had awaken, he had seemed very nervous about something. He had kept on looking towards the sky. My brother had told me that he was I a lot of trouble. He did not want me to tell my mother. I had kept that secret because I had loved my mother so much. At that time, I had thought that he would protect me from anything. Nobody but God can do that. I am very happy that I have God into my life. And I am very happy that I know him. My brother was also married to Marie. She was seven months pregnant, when my stepbrother had died. My stepbrother had come to my mother and fathers which was on a Saturday. He had asked my father what he had wanted for Father's Day. My dad had responded by saying cake and ice- cream. My sister-in-law did not want my brother to get my dad anything. My stepbrother and sister-in-law had started arguing all day. That same day my mother had come to pick me up to go by their house. He had showed me a safe at one time full of money. The safe had $10,000.00 dollars in it. When my brother had gone home the money was gone. The lock was broken, and the money was not there. My brother had hit the mirror with his fist. He was very upset. I didn't know what to do. My sister-in- law had acted like she didn't know what was going on. She was messing around with a lot of young men. I couldn't never find the heart to tell my brother about it. I did not want to cause any more problems into their relationship. At one time he didn't know that was his baby. But the young man looks and act just like my brother. My brother had thrown salt seven times in front and back up him. He didn't want seven years of bad luck. That is what he was told during them days. My sister-in-law had told my stepbrother to pitch it into the river. On Father's Day they had said that my brother had been drinking all day. They had gone to City Park for a picnic. My brother had called my mom and had begged my mother to let me go. My mother did not like them folks. My mother had said that she will beat my ass if I leave the house. She was very strict. I was beaten by extension cords at sometimes. I had to obey my parents at all times. I had a feeling that something was wrong.

When my brother gets drunk, he would not listen to no one. My cousin Don had said that my bother couldn't stand straight. He was just that torn down. My bother will never go into the Mississippi river. He had said that they have too many suck holes into the Mississippi river. The guard had said that he had seemed like they were throwing an object into the water, and someone was jumping after it. My stepbrother brother-in-law had said that my brother had said help one time and went under the water. The guard had tried to find him. But the current was too rough. My stepbrother had gone down with the current. He was way on the other side of the river three days later. My sister-in-law had said that he was trying to go to the Mississippi River all day during Father's Day. My sister-in-law family had come to my mother's house one o' clock in the mourning. She had said that my stepbrother had drowned in the Mississippi river. My brother will never go swimming in no Mississippi river at 10:30pm at night. It was too dark. You can't see anything. We had to wait three days before his body was found. My cousin D better known as Don had found the body on the other side of the river from Tchoupitoulas. My stepbrother body was deep composed. He didn't have an open casket. After the funeral I was in the days of another world. My mother did not let me go. My mother and father had gone to the funeral alone. I was very upset about the situation. My mother and father had known that I had loved my brother dearly. I was only 14th years old at the time of his death. I had kept on answering the phone when it had ranged to see if my brother was going to answer. I was looking out the window for him. I had cried a lot. I had cried so much that I had bags under my eyeballs. I had missed my brother until about a year. I was still grieving a little still. At the age of 15th my baby daddy and his friends had tried to rape me and my best friend. My mother had sent me to go and get some items from the corner store. I had asked my best friend's mother to see if she can come with me; in which she did. We had gone to the store and had seen the guys coming towards us. We had left the stored and had started running by the church by kingley house. I had gotten away but they had caught my best friend. We both were virgins. A school mate was messing around with the guys already. V better known as Valerie had told the guys that were virgins. Someone had passed by the church and that is when they had let my best friend go. Word was around town that they were not finish with us yet. When I had turned to be sixteen years old, I was kind of scared to go outside. I was still a virgin. I don't know about my best friend. I was the only virgin I high school at that time. My girlfriend V better known as Valerie had set me up. She had told my mother that she was giving a party and that all of her friends were invited. My mother had spoken to her parents to make sure that adults was going to be in the house. I didn't know that her mother had left for the evening to a date. JM better known as J, better known as Jim and some of V's friends were there. I, Cristina was also there.

Everyone was drinking Pina Coloda except me. I was kind of on the green side. I didn't know any better. I had wanted to try a drink also. At that time, I was a follower not a leader. I had drunk until I was drunk. I didn't feel very well after five drinks. I had asked V better known as Valerie if I could lay down for a little while. She had said sure. You can go into my bedroom and lay down. Only one thing I could remember is that the room was spinning around. I don't know what was into that drink. I know that it was not a great feeling when I had awakened, I was in so much pain. My baby's daddy had raped me. I was tied to the bed with a sock into my mouth. He had said that it was not going to hurt. I was screaming but no sound. He only had sex with me one time. He had broken my cherry. I was four months pregnant with a son. I, Cristina had gone to the clinic thinking that I had a disease. The young lady at the clinic had said that I was four months pregnant. I was hurting down below. I had the young lady to check it once again, which she did. The place where I had gone was not there anymore after Katrina. That building is no longer there anymore. At this moment, I was very scared. When I had went home, I had stayed in my room for a whole week. I did not want to eat or drink anything. All I could do is cry. I couldn't believe that anyone could do that to anyone. That is a horrible experience to go through. I would not wish that on anyone. My mother had wanted to know what was wrong with me. I had to pretend that nothing was wrong. It had seemed that my mother could see right through me. When I had finally decided to leave the room to try to eat something, my mother was asking me a whole lot of questions. I was always saying that I was alright. One day she had asked me if I was pregnant, and I had told her no. She was about to take me to the doctor to get a checkup. I had gotten sick that week. It had slipped my mother mind. She had forgotten all about the questions that she had asked. I had started gaining weight. It had become a bigger problem now. I didn't know what to do. The doctors had sent some mail to my mother's house. My mother had said that are you pregnant. She had told me do not lie to me. She had put the paper onto the table with the extension cord in her hand. I had finally confessed that I was pregnant. She had asked me who am I pregnant for. I had finally told her that it was for JM better known as Jim. She had said that she has known that something was going on between me and JM better known as Jim. At that moment she didn't know that real reason how I had gotten that way. I didn't want to tell my mother and father at that time because I was scared that they were going to go to prison for the rest of their lives. I didn't want to go to a group like some children around the neighborhood parents did. I had kept that secret form my parents for ten years. I was at the age of 27. I had my son at the age of 17 years old. My mother and father had said that they will help me. I was on my own taking care of my child that I didn't want. My mother and father didn't believe in abortion. My family was very poor at that time. I was too young to take care of a child. I was working and going to school. I was trying to take care of my son on my own.

His father was unfit. He had denied his son until they had taken a D.N.A. The D.N.A. had come back 99°/o that my son was his. My son was at the age of 5 years old. My oldest son Kelvin had graduated from high school with the good Lords help and my parents help. My son had graduated from senior high. He was in the 12th grade. I had to go and get him out of school because they had a route going on into the school. I had gotten him out just in the nick of time. I had to transfer him to another school just to graduate. If he had to do anymore schooling, I don't think he would have never made it. He probably would have dropped out. I am very happy that he had graduated. It was very hard at that time as being a single parent. Kelvin was very proud that he was a graduate. Kelvin and Joshua are nine years apart and five days apart both natural birth. Joshua was the baby and wasn't too expected to be here also. For example: I had worked thirty-two hours that day. I had only wanted to come home to relax. I had fell asleep. I didn't have sex with Joshua's father or anyone for two years. I had awakened and had found my body nude. I had felt someone having sex with me, but I didn't pay it any mind. I was very tied that day. When I had awakened up, I was so mad with big Joshua. I had waited four months to go the doctor. I was not feeling good. The doctor had said that I was pregnant. I had gone to try to get on some birth control pills. I was fighting my whole pregnancy. I did not want another child without someone being my husband. I had Joshua finally. I was still alone. Big Joshua better known as Josh was so drunk most of the time, he didn't have time to help me with little Joshua. I had stayed with Joshua better known as Josh. I had to leave big Joshua better known as Josh. I had tried very hard to stay with him as long as I could. Big Joshua better known as Josh was tearing up my furniture too much. He was very violent when he was drunk. I was twenty-six years old when he had almost shot my brains out. I was sleep in my bed when he had shot through the pillow. That was nothing but God. God is good all of the time. I had cried for days trying to figure out what had happened. But I know that it was the eyes of the good lord. Big Joshua better known as Josh was an alcoholic. He had drunk morning, noon, and night. He was a violent alcoholic. When little Joshua had made two years old I had enough. I could not take it anymore. Big Joshua better known as Josh had locked me into my house for a week without anything to eat. When he had returned back to the house, I had called the police. I could not take it anymore. He was very crazy. I am so happy that I have gotten out of that relationship. I had raised Joshua and Kelvin on my own. They were my pride and joy. Kelvin daddy had raped me at the age of sixth teen years. I was still a young lady. I was a virgin. I did not have a period yet. I had learned to love

Kelvin daddy. I was saving myself for my husband. Which eventually I had gotten married. I had gotten married to the wrong people.

I was married once. Well let me tell you about my husband. My husband was a very hard worker. I had really loved my husband. I was helping my husband help raise his three children. Their mother was on drugs. She was about to lose her children. The state was about to take her children from her. I had gone in the project to pick up the children. They were all crying. I was on section 8th at that time. I had taken all three of his children into my home. I had to raise his three children and my son. The only way the court at that time would accept for him to keep the children he had to get married. At that time, I was not ready to get married. He had told me first we will get married, and then we will get a house later. I was stupid at that time. I had thought that I had learned my lesson. So, I had bought a house with him after we had gotten married. I really didn't want to marry him. He was not my type. I had learned to love him. I was married to Adam for seven years. I was working and going to college. While I was working, he was playing house. I had never told my husband about I knew that he was messing around with my son girlfriend. I had kept it quiet until the end. My ex-husband was very violent. He had said that if I had ever left him again, that he was going to kill me. I didn't do anything to provoke him once I have known. All of this stuff was on my mind. First, he was fucking my son1s girlfriend, and he had wanted to kill me. My husband had stated that as long as I was in his house, that he was going to keep on having sex with me. He was like raping me in my own home. I think that was not fair. One day I had gotten so tied, I had left him for the very last time. Had left him for three times. I had told him this I leave; I am not coming back. He had said no matter what I say or do, I do not want you to leave. One day on October 31st, 2002, he had stated that when was I leaving. He had addressed that he has three hoes waiting to move in. I had told him to give me one month. He had said that I hope it be sooner than that. He had come in the house at 5:00 am November 1st, 2002. He was out all night long with whomever. He had asked me October 31st, 2002, on Halloween night. When everyone had left to go to school, and he had gone to work, I had taken everything out of the house that had belonged to me and had left. It had taken two hours for me, my son, and my daughter-in-law to move my stuff out of that house. It was a new beginning for me. He had come by my mother house with tears into his eyes and had said that I had taken everything and that I had left him. It had started that he had told me to leave. I even took his gun. If the safety would have come off, I think I would be in jail right now. I would have taken out everything that he had brought into my life. I had put down on that four-bedroom home. He had bad credit at that time. The good lord, and I was the one that had helped to get the house and a new van. I had paid for my own divorce. He did not want to give me my divorce. I had told my lawyer to please grant me my divorce. I had gotten my wish. My ex-husband had addressed that he will marry me all over again if he could.

That will never happen up to me. I do not want old news. Adam is still alone living in San Francisco. He had said that he cannot find a good woman like I was. He had said that he wish he cannot find a good woman like I was. He had said that he wish he can replace me, but he can't. He had said that you will not miss a good thing until it is gone. My ex-husband is suffering. I can only say oh well, whatever. I will never be someone who was very abusive, verbal, physical and mental. I am not that kind of girl. I had waited four years before I had dated again. My ex-husband children are doing everything beyond the sun. My ex-husband daughter Calls me from time to time. I have a very good relationship with all of my sister-in-law1s. My ex-husband is living in San Francisco at the present moment. He is buying a house out there. He has a new car and a new house. Sometimes my ex-husband job was very slow. Sometimes he does not work for months that is when it had come in to play for better or worse. I was a good wife. The next husband that I get, it will be from God only. I don't want no any man. I want an honest, caring, and understanding husband. He has to respect and honor our house, and finances. There should be no other woman or man before God and us. All of my ex-husband children have strayed away. Lisa better known as Apples is in Atlantic, Dalia better known as Queen is in New Orleans wondering from house to house, and Alvin better known as Mike is still living with his dad in San

Francisco. Lisa better known as peaches is six months pregnant. Dalia better known as princess has a little boy, And Alvin do not have any children. They are all living a life of their own. Joshua's father is an alcoholic. He is still drinking. Kelvin's father is going to AAA meetings @ the present moment. He was always on drugs without my knowledge. At one time he had tried to get me to take some drugs by caging me into the drug house. I had just run into some bad relationships in my life time. I will try to be a little bit more careful from now on. I do wish in every way that I was still married, but not to someone who does not take pride in a relationship. I would like someone better and over and beyond my old flames. Sometimes I get so lonely, I have no one to cuddle up with. I only have a lonely bed to lie in. One day I will not have to go through this. When I do find me a real man with the good lord's help, I will always hold on to him. As long as he is doing his part, I will always try to do my part. I have learned my lesson for being alone so long. I remember during Katrina when I had lost everything. I had left New Orleans on August 28, 2005. I had returned back to New Orleans September 9th, 2005. I had returned back to New Orleans to nothing. Here is when I began my story during Katrina. All I could do was just cry. By Cristina who was a Katrina victim, I know a lot of people have lost a lot of family and friends. I will tell my story. I was working with 32 lockdown patients. I had evacuated from New Orleans to a nursing home with the patients, staff, and nurses. My ex old man had rescued my children.

They would have drowned if it was not for the good lord or my ex old man. My job had told me that I would be making plenty of money during the storm; that was all lies. My job had told me that they were going to give each employee $500.00 dollars, and we were going to a hotel. All that stuff that we were told were all lies. We all were in an abandoned building down the street from the job. I only had two dollars in my pocket when I had left New Orleans. The nursing home was only operating from a generator. The staff were stealing the patient's money. They were taking the patient credit cards and using them. The employees had to survive on their own. We had to move to another nursing home. The staff that was stealing are still at the job. We had to find a way to get to our jobs once they had made a decision to move to San Francisco. I have signed the paper, but I have never gone. I had lost my memory. I didn't even know if I had a family anymore. My father had died on December 4th, 2005, because of stress. I couldn't get any connection through the phone system at that time. Even though I had lost my memory, I was still taking care of the patients. Someone had put guns to our heads down the street from the job three times. I had worker out there for a whole month until I had decided to call it quits. I had left New Orleans on August 27th, 2005. I had returned back to New Orleans October 10, 2005. My house was not livable. I was in a shelter. That was after I had left the job. I had found out where my ex old man was and my children. I could not talk. All I could do was just cry. I didn't remember who they were. I had gone to see my home to try to salvage my stuff, but it could not be salvaged. I had just fell on the ground. My house was one inch of water from the roof for a whole month. I had only had three days of clothing. I think God each and every day for Habitat for Humanity and for Mike Hastings for helping me. I have been selected to get my own home. Mike Hastings realtor had keys waiting for me when I have arrived in Hammond as of 11/16/2005. I appreciate who all have helped me and my family. Only thing that Beacon Light in Hammond had done for me by making me feel at home. I am still struggling a little bit. I have to try to get my $2,000.00 down payment for my house. I show can tell you this, when you are breaking no one is there to help you. When you get on your feet once again, looks like everyone knows you. God has brought me out of this one. You wait until I shine. I had to spend all of my FEMA money on the left-over bills that was left behind by Katrina in New Orleans and to get a place to live for me and my family. And I also had to loan my ex old man $6,000.00 which was not paid back. The FEMA money had left me with nothing. He had said that he was going to pay me back. He had brought a truck with the money that I have loaned him. I wish the best luck to all that have survived from Hurricane Katrina. I know that I have lost everything material wise, but I thank God that I haven't lost my dignity and sense of humor. My ex old man had caught HIV after Katrina. He had tried to hide the information from me. You have to be very careful in this world. He still hasn't told anyone. I happen to be looking for some information in the house and had locked up on this information; He still do not know that I have this information.

Thank God that we have been using protective during the three years before Katrina. He was telling my children that their mother was dead. When my son's and grandchildren had knew that I was alive, you could have seen their face. I had to search for my sister and brothers. My mother, one of my brothers, and father had to be rescued from a helicopter. My father, mother, and one of my brothers were all in Oakdale. My father was dying. My father had died of stress. My father had colon cancer, and he also had diabetics. That had taken a toll on me. I will just hope and pray for everyone who had survived everything. I will just advise everyone to be strong. I am a survivor. I have a three-bedroom house, a 2011 Altima which was brand new. I am about to get my M.B.A. I will tell everyone like my dad had said before he had died to keep your head up for everyone and everything. I know that no one can steal my joy. I have gotten my M.B.A. I had graduated with honors. After that it was another downfall in my life. My mother has gotten diagnosed with ovarian cancer. That was another ordeal in my life. I was praying each day for her to recover. My mother had lost a lot of weight, lost her hair, and could not remember anything. My sisters and brothers had to comfort my mother including me. I am the one had known something was wrong with my mother when there was a file Oder when I had gone into town. She is in readmission. Her hair has grown back, and she also has gained her weight back. Sometimes in life you go through so much. I had thought I had met someone in my life who was a real man. But our friendship was nothing but lies. I had dated him for four years. He was using me all of the time. For example: I had helped him get some jobs in place. When he had lost his job, I had helped him to get unemployment. That is just the kind of person that I am. I love helping others no matter what. I have met someone in my life now who makes me so happy. He is a very passionate young man. I need everything that he gives me. He makes me smile even when I do not have the place and feeling to do so. I know we have just met, but it seems like I have known him forever. He does not have much to give, but he cares about me and most of the time he has a heart. I am tired of searching. I just want to be happy. I put God first in everything I do. And I thank everyone out there for the encouragement and motivation.

ABOUT THE AUTHOR

My name is Ella Jean Jackson. I was born Tylertown Mississippi Walthall County. I reside in Ponchatoula Louisiana. I am Fifty-six years of age. I have a B.S. in nursing. I also have an M.B.A in business Administration. I have two sons ages are Thirty-nine and Thirty years. I have five grand kids. I am working as a C.N.A right now. I have been working in that field for 34 years. I can't work as a nurse because I did not take the state board. I am an author who you all know by now. No, I am not going back to schooling. But I know one thing that I will pursue in my MBA degree and see where that degree will lead me and guide me into the next level.

www.ingramcontent.com/pod-product-compliance
Lightning Source LLC
LaVergne TN
LVHW040204080526
838202LV00042B/3318